Monday
MARRIAGE

Monday
MARRIAGE

Celebrating the Ordinary

Gerald W. Kaufman
L. Marlene Kaufman

Foreword by Victor and Marie Stoltzfus

Herald Press
Scottdale, Pennsylvania
Waterloo, Ontario

Library of Congress Cataloging-in-Publication Data
Kaufman, Gerald W., 1939-
  Monday marriage : celebrating the ordinary / Gerald W. Kaufman,
L. Marlene Kaufman.
      p. cm.
  Includes bibliographical references.
  ISBN 0-8361-9304-0 (pbk. : alk. paper)
  1. Marriage—Religious aspects—Christianity. 2. Spouses—Religious life.
I. Kaufman, L. Marlene, 1939- II. Title.
  BV4596.M3K38 2005
  248.8'44—dc22
                                                              2005015571

MONDAY MARRIAGE
Copyright © 2005 by Herald Press, Scottdale, Pa. 15683
  Published simultaneously in Canada by Herald Press,
  Waterloo, Ont. N2L 6H7. All rights reserved
Library of Congress Catalog Card Number: 2005015571
International Standard Book Number: 0-8361-9304-0
Printed in the United States of America
Book design by Sandra Johnson
Cover design by Sans Serif Inc.

12 11 10 09 08 07 06 05   10 9 8 7 6 5 4 3 2 1

To order or request information, please call
1-800-759-4447 (individuals); 1-800-245-7894 (trade).
Web site: www.heraldpress.com

*To Emery and Mattie Cender and
to Calvin and Margaret Kaufman, our parents,
who were shining examples of Monday Marriage.
Their simple, unpretentious lives displayed to us
the real meaning of marriage.*

Contents

Foreword

William Mather, an elderly professor at Penn State University, used to shake his head and say, "There is nothing so uncommon as common sense."

Jerry and Marlene Kaufman write about marriage with a rare common sense distilled from decades of counseling. What is uncommon in this book is their remarkable capacity to connect the pain of troubled marriages to toxicity in the larger social and cultural setting. We marry and try to stay married in a society that is polluted with many distortions and outright lies.

The view of marriage that you will discover in these pages also requires the courage to discern and reject much of the marriage advice mediated by pop psychology, celebrity worship and even frothy religion.

At times Jerry and Marlene are combative in tone. They are gentle people but have strong convictions because they have seen so much wreckage. In the privacy of counseling sessions they have witnessed the agony of spouses who have built on unstable foundations, kind of like those multimillion-dollar coastal California homes that come sliding down a hillside: the architecture is pleasing, but sunshine and an ocean view are powerless to stop the collapse.

In this book, the Kaufmans invite us to take a look at marriage as a spiritual endeavor, to view with awe the mystery and grandeur of how our Creator made us human.

The positive side of this book affirms marriage romance and passion. Precisely because the Kaufmans know marriage can be delightful, they want to persuade us to carve out time and space to nourish our marriages. They warn us that good things like work, entertainment and personal hobbies may need to be trimmed back so that our marriages don't choke from lack of air. They locate their idealism for marriage in the ordinary stuff of a husband's whistling and a wife's apple fritters. They don't scold with Bible verses but are profoundly biblical in responding to the challenge of covenant and God's gifts of love and grace. With grand simplicity, the Kaufmans urge us to reduce what we expect *from* our marriages, as we expand what we commit *to* our marriages.

We recommend this book for engaged couples, for married couples who are troubled or doing well, for marriage counselors, for pastors and for church libraries. The book is fresh and original, even though it speaks to a topic as ancient as the Garden of Eden.

—*Victor and Marie Stoltzfus*
Goshen, Indiana

Preface

We know there are already too many books on the subject of marriage, not to mention the numerous magazine articles, videos, TV and radio programs on the subject. And let's not forget the retreats and seminars. Without a doubt the market has been saturated. If people want information, there is plenty available, all the way from the highly technical and scientific to deeply personal stories of dramatic marital recoveries. A virtual smorgasbord of advice awaits couples.

So, why one more book? The first reason is personal. Marlene and I have been marriage counselors for many years. As we enter the last phase of our careers, we feel compelled to say something about what we have learned. The people who have invited us into their private lives reveal important truths. Sitting by marital bedsides, we have often served as hospice workers to dying marriages. We have looked into the eyes of forsaken spouses or abandoned children whose grief is impossible to ignore. The burden is even heavier when a divorce is unnecessary and preventable.

The second reason for writing this book is professional. We have a growing conviction that much of the advice being offered about marriage is misleading. Some of it may even be harmful. Although the intentions of the advice-givers may be honorable, we believe much of it misses the point. It is frequently filled with exaggerations and misinformation. This advice sets a standard that is impossible for most people to attain. Some of it promotes individual-ism in marriage more than cooperation. We hope our book will offer a different point of view to readers.

The third reason for writing is to reassure couples that their marriage isn't necessarily in trouble even though they may experience times of anger, breakdowns in communi-cation, or sexual disappointments. For many that is hard to do when the popular culture encourages perfection in marriage. But being critical of the intricacies of marriage is like standing too close to a van Gogh painting: all that can be seen are crude brush strokes. With marriage, as with a great painting, we must step back a bit to see the real beau-ty of the big picture.

Most of all, marriage is about spiritual maturity. Using the metaphor "Monday Marriage," we invite you to see marriage as a sacred union built around truthfulness and reality, not trivialized by a culture of superficiality and sec-ularity. This is a book that advocates *giving to* marriage much more than *getting from* marriage. Our book is about marriage, to be sure, but it is about much more than that. Perhaps more than anything, it invites sacrifice, humility, and honoring God by serving our spouse, our children, and others.

Following the pattern of our previous book, *Freedom Fences: How to Set Limits That Free You to Enjoy Your Marriage and Family* (Herald Press, 1999), we have cho-sen not to use stories from individual clients. Even if we had their written permission, to us it would seem like exploitation. People's lives often change and the details that are permanently placed in print might be hurtful at a later point. And quite frankly, we don't feel right about using personal stories in ways that are self-serving. So we use composite stories, all of them truthful, but none from a particular couple.

We write in a style that we hope is readable and accessible. We have attempted to keep this book from sounding like a psychological treatise. We quote some experts, but not many from the usual cadre. It is our belief that marriage has been contaminated by too much high-sounding verbiage. Sometimes those words seem to be driven more by selling books or creating celebrity than by genuine compassion for vulnerable couples.

Most of all, it is our intention to invite couples to set aside the trivial, the exaggerated, and the pompous, and enjoy a marriage that is richly ordinary; a relationship that is content with life's frailties and bursting with the hope that tomorrow will be much like today. And today is good! It's Monday.

We want to give special thanks to those who guide us on this walk. Our editor, Dr. Victor Stoltzfus—with his insightful wife, Marie, looking over his shoulder—gave us invaluable advice to keep us on the path. In their critiques, they suggested improvements—both large and small—that have greatly enhanced what we have said. Along the way their gentle nudges to keep moving helped enormously when we were met with a blank screen and an empty mind. They kept us inspired, energized, and humored by quoting lyrics from the folk songs of our youth. On one occasion they even wrote poetry to lift our spirits. Given the fact that this book is about marriage, Marie balanced out the ticket with her pleas to warm up the text and to make *Monday Marriage* rich in joyfulness.

Herald Press director Levi Miller supported us in our somewhat unconventional approach. We may not have always been as clear as we could have been in explaining the book to him. We confess that our ideas matured as the book was written. It really was a work-in-progress up to the very end. But Levi hung on and we appreciate that.

And many thanks to Michael Degan, editor for Herald Press, who helped us get this book ready for print. His help was invaluable.

And for the support from our family, Brent and Cheryl, Nate and Cathy, Anne and Todd, Nina and Craig, who sometimes had to put up with our computer face when they dropped in. And for the patience of our grandchildren, Keri, Alyssa, Caleb, Ashley, Lara, Adam, Taylor, Seth, Mary, Lauren, and Isaac, who deserved more of our time than we could give them. We promise to make it up.

Most of all to my co-writer, Marlene, with whom I celebrate nearly forty-five years of Monday marriage, thank you. Indeed, many thanks! It has been a life rich in its commonness. Made so by her willingness to tolerate our differences. By her steadiness when I am unsteady. Patient when I am impatient. We learn every day from each other. As much as anything this book reveals *our* marriage. If credit is due much goes to her. I am a lucky man. Or more correctly I am a blessed man. Thanks be to God!

—*Gerald W. Kaufman*
June 2005

1

Introduction to Monday Marriage

"Sarah, my dear wife of thirty years, died over two years ago. I still tremble when I dwell on her passing. I did not think she would expire first. It may have been consumption. Whatever the cause, she is gone. There is nothing to be gained by questioning the Lord's timing. How I miss her cakes with burnt sugar. She always knew what to say to encourage me. It is a mystery how a wife can become commonplace, as ordinary as an apple or corn fritter, until suddenly she is gone. Then the appetite for the fritter takes over. Sinking my teeth into the apple is all I could dwell on."

—*Amish minister, Isaac*[1]

What's a Monday Marriage?

Even though many "experts" suggest marriage can—and should—be terrific, the truth is that most marriages are rather ordinary. So ordinary that we call them "Monday Marriage." Monday because that's when the day-to-day routine sets the real tone for the marriage. It is when spouses take off their masks and display all of their warts and idiosyncrasies. Sometimes Monday people are grumpy. At other times they are aloof. Often they are boringly predictable. Monday people have long ago stopped trying to impress each other. They have given up expecting euphoria in their relationship. Their marriage isn't fueled by adrenaline or by fantasy. It doesn't need to be. Monday spouses are happy with what they have because they know it is the real thing.

Spouses in Monday Marriage don't spend much time analyzing their relationship. They are more concerned with getting the kids on the school bus or having enough money for the next mortgage payment. Monday people accept the ups and downs in their relationship as a normal part of life and aren't that interested in finding a number, letter, or a name for their personalities. When they are annoyed with each other, they don't panic or look for an exit strategy.

Instead of chasing after unattainable dreams, Monday people learn to dream realistically. They don't labor over their marriage as a perpetual project to be "working on." They have long ago stopped living with "if only" and "what if" and accept "what is" as sufficient. They have both good and bad memories, a willing acceptance of the present, and realistic hopes for the future.

Being ordinary doesn't mean that Monday people live a dull life. They don't resemble the straight-laced couple who stand with pitch fork in hand staring out at a somber world in the well-known painting "American Gothic." They celebrate birthdays with gusto, indulge themselves by occasionally going to their favorite restaurant, and may even get a bit extravagant by taking an exotic vacation. They experience moments of romance and passion and unexpected surprise. Laughter and tears come on occasion. Their relationship is especially rich because they don't allow themselves to be influenced by the world around them. Monday people experience good times in simple, elegant ways. Poet Jeff Gundy refers to these times as, "small beauties, austere joys, and severe pleasures."[2]

If your perch is high, you have much further to fall than if your perch is low. The amount of choice we now have in most aspects of our lives contributes to high expectations.[3]

—*Barry Schwartz*

Now we want it all—a partner who reflects our taste and status, who sees us for who we are, who loves us for all the "right" reasons, who helps us become the person we want to be. We've done away with a rigid social order, adopting instead an even more onerous obligation: the mandate to find a perfect match. Anything short of this ideal prompts us to ask: Is this all there is? Am I as happy as I should be? Could there be somebody out there who's better for me? As often as not, we answer "yes" to that last question and fall victim to our own great expectations. ....The reality is that few marriages . . . consistently live up to this ideal.[4]

—*Polly Shulman*

Expecting Too Much from Marriage

Many people question their relationship when they are told marriage should be more. Much more! That it should be filled with passion and romance. That it will be a "great relationship" if they have the proper communication skills and a good understanding of each other's personality. According to this type of advice, couples will be "catapulted to new heights" and will live in virtual "ecstasy" if only they try hard enough. In our "feel good, follow your dreams" culture, couples are told to expect a great marriage if they undertake the proper steps. In this environment, some expect to have all of their "needs" met by their spouse. They see marital "happiness" as a *right*.

Unfortunately, much of this information creates illusions that sow seeds of discord. Most of it is impossible to apply to marriage on a day-to-day basis. But because it sounds convincing, many couples try. After all, who wouldn't wish for the passion of the early years? Or to have the dramatic "cures" that the couples on the talk shows describe? And to have a "soul mate" for a spouse, who wouldn't want that?

When some people fail to reach these impossible levels, they begin to believe their marriage is doomed. Many question whether they should stay together. Some enter a "commitment limbo" staying with their spouse while at the same time keeping "one stealthy foot out the door of their hearts." According to John Jacobs, that is because "We live in a society that promotes so many powerful lies about marriage, so many misunderstandings, myths and fairy tales that have become so deeply entrenched in our minds that we are rarely able to approach marriage with reasonable expectations."[5]

For some individuals, marital unhappiness may be influenced by what psychologist Barry Schwartz calls, "the tyranny of choice." When we have unlimited choices for everything from toothpaste to magazines, the stage is set for dissatisfaction. Having so many choices, it is hard to know if we have chosen our mate correctly. As strange as it may sound, having too many choices can make us unhappy, even with our marriage! Schwartz believes it contributes "to an epidemic of unhappiness" that is "spreading through modern society."

This epidemic encourages attitudes of superficiality and restlessness. Sometimes it is seen in people who hop from one church to another in search of spiritual excitement. Or in people who frequently change jobs to find personal fulfillment. For others it is in pursuing one diet plan after another or cosmetic surgery to change their appearance. In this environment, marriage is just another "choice" that is continuously being considered. When the relationship does not meet our expectations, it too can be set aside for a new one. Perhaps the half-life of contentment is getting shorter. In our hyperactive society, even marriage is plagued with an "attention deficit." Let's look at some of the ways we expect too much from marriage:

For many couples the problems start at the wedding. The average wedding today costs more than $20,000. Many weddings resemble proms and coronations more than a sacred event. It is no surprise that couples get the wrong idea about marriage. Unrealistic weddings can produce unrealistic marriages.

Couples are expected to be experts in understanding their personalities. While they're expected to make adjustments to each other's personalities based on tests, categories, and technical insights, many of the instruments used to interpret personality are quite subjective and can be misused by the couple. Sometimes this leads to conflict that is a first step on the path to divorce. Many people feel let down when they believe they aren't married to their "soul mate" or when the spouse doesn't change enough to meet expectations.

Many couples believe that intense, frequent, and passionate sex will be a constant part of their marriage. They ignore the fact that jobs, children, and other responsibilities take time and energy away from the bedroom. In addition, they don't want to face the reality that partner familiarity changes sexual mystique.

Couples hear that "good communication" will give them a strong marriage. In reality spouses communicate very differently. Even though they may learn certain "techniques," it is hard to use them continually, partly because they can seem somewhat artificial. Often their communication doesn't measure up to the "standard" they hoped for.

Giving Too Little to Marriage

We live in a world that encourages *getting* much more than *giving*, and that is more concerned with chasing dreams than being at peace with reality. In his inaugural speech in 1961, President John F. Kennedy raised this issue in reference to citizenship. He told the nation, "Ask not what your country can do for you. Ask what you can do for your country." Jesus also spoke to this condition by warning us that ". . . many who are first will be last, and the last will be first" (Mark 10:31). Sociologist Don Kraybill says that people who choose to go against the popular culture live in an "upside-down kingdom."

Thus we have come to expect too much *from* marriage but are unwilling to give what a marriage needs to stay strong. Marriage prospers when we are realistic and make sacrifices for the good of the relationship. Some of the ways we give too little to marriage include the following:

We view marriage as a temporary legal contract, not a life-long spiritual covenant. Monday couples reject the culture's tendency to ". . . park on the border of the relationship," as psychotherapist Terrance Real describes it. Instead, they keep both feet in the marriage and make a life-long commitment to give to each other "in sickness and in health." In Monday Marriage, covenant is a sacred promise made to God. It is much more than a legal contract to be set aside when it fails to meet personal expectations. Monday people accept imperfections in their spouse and don't demand unreasonable changes. They learn the lost art of forgiveness.

We place our jobs ahead of the needs of our marriage. Jobs can be hazardous to marriage. They place heavy demands on the time and energy of spouses. The workplace can also strain the loyalty of a spouse. Increasingly the workplace is squeezing marriage into the margin. Spouses are often like ships passing in the night, especially when the jobs require a lot of overtime, travel, or shift work. The workplace also is becoming a threat to marriage by creating close relationships with fellow workers. Sometimes those friendships lead to affairs. In other situations, they only divert the focus away from the spouse. For marriage to survive, couples need to protect their relationship from the hazards of the workplace.

Couples are harmed by too much busyness. Recreation, hobbies, and children's activities often take us away from each other. Church and community programs as well as volunteer commitments add to the overload. Increasingly, activities are filling family schedules to the point of exhaustion. We further deplete the marriage by watching too much TV or spending too much time on the computer. Giving back to marriage means eliminating excessive activities in order to preserve time for each other.

The Goodness About Monday

When Gerald's father died at sixty-eight, his mother grieved. One of the things she missed most when he was gone was his whistling. Dad always whistled. At work, in the car, when he was happy, sad, whenever. It was a voice that spoke loudly to Mom and to the rest of us. The silence that took over when the whistling ended was painful, much like what Minister Isaac experienced when his wife died. Whistling and apple fritters belong to Monday Marriage. They are at the heart of what really joins us in this wonderful relationship called marriage.

Monday Marriage is *good*. Much better than the hyped-up version that is for sale today. It is good because it is based in reality, genuineness, and on God's original architecture for marriage. We need to celebrate the treasure we have and stop looking for something better. Popular ideas of happiness only mislead and confuse us. Genuine happiness and real intimacy are only a step away. We invite you to take that first step as you read the chapters that follow. The journey isn't as hard or complicated as some "experts" would have us believe. To achieve Monday Marriage we need to give up fantasies and lower our expectations. At the same time we choose to make our marriage—and our commitment to the Creator of marriage—more important than anything else. That is what Monday Marriage is all about.

Part One

Expecting Less

2

Weddings: Starting Marriage the Right Way

The first day of marriage usually starts with a wedding. To some extent it is a predictor for what is to follow. How couples—and their families—handle the wedding can reveal a great deal about their character, their priorities, and their relationship. The wedding can establish patterns that either burden or strengthen the marriage.

The Importance of Weddings

Weddings are very important public events in every country, culture, and religion. The costumes, rituals, and traditions may differ, but weddings are always times of celebration. Even in less affluent cultures, families stage colorful, elaborate ceremonies. While Amish weddings are generally more conservative, the "wedding season" (usually in the Fall) is a time for frenzied sewing, tidying up the property where the wedding takes place, feasting, and visiting.

Indeed, the wedding is the biggest event in which most of us will ever plan or participate. Relatives and friends come from near and far. A small army of people are called on to help couples get married. Bridesmaids and attendants join them in the walk up and down the aisle. Parents escort them to the altar, light the unity candle, and give verbal assent to the marriage. Nieces and nephews serve as flower girls and ring bearers. Best men give toasts at the reception. Musicians give miniature concerts. Ministers do their part to make the wedding legally and spiritually valid. And this says nothing about the professionals who are hired to take pictures, prepare the banquet, and perform many other services. Many weddings are so complicated that they require coordinators to keep the events moving smoothly.

But have weddings become too elaborate, and do they focus on the wrong things? More importantly, do excessive weddings have a negative influence on marriage? Decisions about weddings are often driven by adrenaline, slick sales pitches from consultants, and competition among peers and, sometimes, parents. In a society that encourages self-indulgence, it is hard to maintain reasonable boundaries. Extravagance in weddings is fueled by the myth that couples deserve the best regardless of the cost. Some justify the expense as a down payment for a "good marriage."

Getting Married Versus Being Married

When weddings are extravagant they can cause couples to *expect too much from their marriage*. Couples are sometimes more caught up with *getting married* than they are with *being married*. When the excitement of the wedding wears off, it can be hard to adjust to the reality that follows. Within a short time, the day-to-day routine takes over, and many couples aren't prepared for the ordinariness that follows. The dramatic buildup to the wedding is replaced with the realities of Monday mornings. Their parents, the bridal party, musicians, guests, food preparers, and the guests have gone on with their lives. The flowers have wilted. Gifts have to be put away. Thank you notes need to be written. The curtain has been closed on the drama.

For the first time, the couple is alone in an undramatic world. They quickly become aware in their aloneness and that they are now dependent on each other to make their marriage work. They discover that their wedding hasn't automatically brought them the happiness they expected. In fact, the opposite may be the case.

It is somewhat ironic—perhaps not entirely coinciden-tal—that while weddings are becoming more expensive, marriages are lasting for shorter times. New information indicates that 20 percent of all marriages end within the first five years; 25 percent of these failures happen within the first two years.

Author Pamela Paul names these "starter marriages." She compares them to the "starter homes" that many peo-ple buy early in their marriage and later replace with larger, fancier homes. In a similar way she believes some people regard the first marriage as a temporary one that will also be replaced when a "better" one comes along. Unfortunately, 65 percent of second marriages end in divorce. Many of these people won't succeed in their "dream marriage" either.

Weddings and Costs

Some people can afford to have an expensive wedding. Either the couple has enough money themselves or their parents do. They feel entitled to whatever kind of wedding they choose. They may even justify the expense believing that their special wedding will be a good investment, per-haps like a down payment on their marriage. Weddings can also be social statements intended to impress other people. There is enormous peer pressure to have weddings that look good, speak well of the family, and give pleasure to the bride and groom.

There is no evidence that extravagant weddings guarantee anything. Money can't buy intimacy. It may purchase temporary euphoria but not permanent security. It may impress people on the wedding day but lose its power when the couple faces the realities of daily living. These weddings can create the illusion that marriage is about *things* and not about *commitment, sacrifice, and service.* But the couple that can afford a fancy wedding may pay a significant emotional and spiritual cost.

More typically couples spend beyond what they or their parents can afford. They also feel the pressure to have a "nice wedding." So parents make sacrifices in other parts of their lives and borrow money to purchase the wedding the couple wants. Often the bride and groom are swept off their feet by wedding enthusiasm and are unaware of the burden they are placing on their parents.

In fact, in the weeks and months before the wedding, it is common for the couple to have conflicts with their families over finances and wedding plans. If their best friend has eight bridesmaids they want at least that many. If "everybody else" is getting married at a lakeshore chapel, they don't want to look cheap by having their wedding in an ordinary-looking church. In a world of too many choices, the possibilities for weddings today are virtually limitless.

Greg and Sheri are one such couple. They met after college as young urban professionals in their late twenties. Both had high-paying jobs requiring fifty to sixty hours per week. Wanting to get a head start before they were married, they bought a condo. But the mortgage was so high they couldn't afford their dream wedding, so they turned to her parents for help.

Sheri's parents had a limited income and couldn't afford the high-priced wedding she wanted. They lived in a very modest home and drove old cars. They were able to eke out a meager existence from the mother's modest income and the father's disability benefits. But feeling obligated to give their daughter the wedding she desired, the parents took out a large loan. Three years later, with a sizeable balance still due on the loan, the father died. At that time Greg and Sheri were still working very long hours and were struggling with day-care costs for their new baby. They discovered that neither their dream wedding nor their high-paying jobs brought them happiness. Instead, they were fatigued, irritable, and "falling out of love." Their wedding didn't bring security to their marriage.

The Wedding Industry

It is no accident that weddings have become so expensive. An industry has sprung up to create excess. Wedding consultants often have more influence than the parents or the church. They seize on this period of high emotion to create fantasies and sell their wares to vulnerable couples and their parents. The costuming gets more elaborate and the price keeps going up. The flowers are more exotic, and the food more haute cuisine. There are even consultants who specialize in planning overseas weddings.

We recently witnessed a newly married couple being whisked away from their church by helicopter. Perhaps it was a way to get "higher" than they already were. Maybe to speed them away to an airport where they could fly to an exotic island. But their excesses aren't unusual. Some couples rent stretch Hummers to accommodate the bridal party. Others come in horse drawn carriages. Weddings take place in hot air balloons, on cruise ships, underwater, and many other unusual places. Such weddings have become part circus, part coronation, and part exhibitionism. But they do nothing to contribute positively to the marital relationship.

People who marry with such superficiality tend to view their commitment to marriage the same way.

Other Kinds of Excesses

While most weddings are traditional and more restrained, many suffer from a lack of depth. They have music that is filled with sentimentality more appropriate for a senior prom than for a wedding. Ministers can get caught up in offering oversimplified or misleading advice in their homilies. Too frequently, their words to the couple include popular psychological clichés about communication, conflict, or sex and romance. Those who remember the minister's words discover that in the real world, the advice often doesn't help much.

Some couples have nontraditional weddings that are "earthy" and inexpensive. They stage them in the backyard, in their favorite park, by streams, or in other "free" places. While their intentions may be noble and the outcomes can be beautiful, the downside is that distractions often take away from the sacredness of the wedding. Outdoor weddings can be held hostage to rain, mosquitoes, wind, heat or cold, highway traffic, and a host of other uncontrollable circumstances. These weddings can add extra work and worry for the family. And the bride and groom may get so caught up in the complexities of the setting that they miss the main point for the day.

In some marriages the problems start in the weeks before the wedding. Bachelor and bachelorette parties are often crude, profane events that do immense harm. Some involve heavy alcohol use. Others use strip-tease artists to provide a "last-fling" before marriage. Male friends have been known to pay for a prostitute to entertain the groom. The message to the couple is that they have a right to a night of pleasure before they get "tied down." While these activities may be more common with secular marriages, it is unfortunate that they have crept into the Christian community as well. In either case they create twisted ideas about sex, intimacy, and responsibility.

Changing the Wedding Culture

Monday Marriage begins with Monday weddings. Inflated weddings produce inflated expectations. When reality is missing from the wedding, it is difficult to develop in the marriage. Couples need to discover *new ways* to get married, ways that flow smoothly throughout the engagement, the wedding, honeymoon, and into the marriage. The present wedding culture disconnects couples from reality. It has brides and grooms playing out roles that bear little resemblance to who they will need to be as spouses. To claim meaningful reality in Monday Marriage, the following approach toward weddings may be helpful:

Discover deeper meaning for marriage by cutting wedding costs. This can be done by having fewer attendants, reception meals that are simpler, guest lists that are shorter, flowers that are less elaborate, and photography and videography that is more reasonable. Simplified weddings reduce stress for the couple, allowing them to experience the joy intended for their wedding day. It puts them in touch with the true meaning of marriage. As a bonus for their restraint the money saved can be used to pay off debt, make a down payment on a house, or to start a savings account. Weddings can be celebrated with an elegant simplicity that reflects genuine beauty rather than burdensome excess.

Make the wedding an expression of sensitivity and thoughtfulness. The bride and groom will demonstrate respect and sacrifice to each other through restraint. They will show sensitivity to family members by incorporating them meaningfully into the wedding. They will be aware of the needs of the guests by providing a comfortable setting for them and by moving the events along in a timely way. During the reception the toasts and personal sharing will be meaningful to more than just the bride and groom.

In displaying this kind of sensitivity, the couple recognizes that the day doesn't belong to them alone. They acknowledge that they are an extension of their family, friends, and church community. Even though the bride and groom are center stage, they need to handle their temporary celebrity with maturity.

Couples should experience the wedding as an act of worship. The ceremony honors God, the creator of marriage. The people in attendance are not mere spectators but are participants in a holy moment. If the wedding includes music that has spiritual dignity, it will be meaningful to the couple and the people who attend. The rituals and symbols should display submission to God and to each other. Pastors are empowered to be more than mere role players. They can help shape the wedding and speak boldly about the spiritual foundations of marriage. When weddings are worshipful, couples begin their life together in the right spirit.

The wedding should flow seamlessly into marriage. The wedding is, after all, the first day of the marriage. When pageantry distorts weddings, it is much harder for couples to face Monday morning with realism. The wedding isn't a separate event that stands out uniquely from the days that will follow, but serves as a good preparation for building a relationship that has integrity. Weddings with the right balance provide couples with a soft landing in marriage.

Joyful Weddings

God intends for weddings to be joyful. Jesus assisted in bringing joy to the wedding at Cana. But there is a difference between *real joy* and the *joy* that is purchased with money. *Real joy* comes when couples are united through the mystery of this sacred bond. Dennis Covington suggests, "Mystery is not the absence of meaning, but the presence of more meaning than we can comprehend."[6] When mystery happens we get goose bumps, cry and smile at the same time. In some ways the moment seems too private to be shared but too holy to miss.

These moments are uniquely spiritual times when the world stands still and when words aren't enough to explain what is happening. In some ways they compare to the birth of new life and to spiritual rebirth. Weddings are so sacred and so filled with emotion that they deserve to be protected from commercial influences. Monday spouses know they are receiving a priceless wedding treasure. They will—on their wedding day and in the marriage that follows—be good stewards of this gift.

3

Accepting Personality Differences

Pam went to her attorney to begin the process of terminating her marriage. She stated as her reason, "We're just too different." The attorney pressed for details about her husband, Mike, expecting to hear the usual complaints. Often when wives seek divorce it is because the husband is having an affair or is abusive. Sometimes it is from spending too much time at work or in recreation. But the attorney was surprised to hear that it was none of these things. In fact, Pam admitted that her husband is faithful, gentle, and spends time with her and their children. By most people's standards he would be considered a good husband and father.

When pressed for more information, Pam struggled to justify her decision. Finally she disclosed she is giving up because she and her husband are not a good personality match. She described herself as outgoing and her husband as more reserved. She talks a lot. He very little. She is a risk taker and he more cautious. In her view, the marriage has gone flat and she has no interest in reviving it. In fact, she recalled the words of her pastor in one of their premarriage counseling sessions. "Your personality tests," he told them, "show that you are quite different and you will have to work hard to overcome those differences." He gave them some technical-sounding categories that seemed to back up his advice.

Those words followed her during ten years of marriage, and the labels from the test have stuck with her as clearly as her name. The test identified her as an extrovert and him as an introvert. Additionally, it suggested that she is enthusiastic, versatile, and good at communication. On the negative side, it warned that she might have trouble completing projects.

Mike's test said that he is quiet, gentle, and seeks harmony. However, because he may feel strongly about his beliefs, the tests suggest that he could appear to be rigid. It has been very hard for Pam to not see Mike as defective when she thinks about these labels. More than just being interesting descriptions, they jump out at her every time she tries to initiate a conversation and he responds slowly. She has little patience when his brief answers conflict with her ideas. Or when she wants to vacation in new places and he prefers returning to familiar ones. Pam believes Mike has some personality weaknesses that can't be changed and that she deserves someone who is more compatible with her.

Pam is convinced she made a mistake in marrying Mike. The personality tests they took provide her with the proof she needs. Besides, the pastor warned them about their differences. Now she wants to move on with her life because she no longer loves him. Even though Mike promises to change she is convinced that the differences are "irreconcilable." She feels entitled to a better match with someone who can bring out the best in her.

Differences Can be Challenging

All couples have differences and to some degree are "incompatible." Indeed, we tend to be drawn to people who are different from us in many ways. People who are too much like us don't interest us. There is a certain kind of mystery, intrigue, and even comfort in the differences we bring to each other. On the practical side, we often marry people who create balance in the relationship. Persons who are more emotional tend to marry less emotional mates. Spenders often choose savers. Worriers are drawn to non-worriers.

So the issue isn't so much that spouses are different. It is what we do with those differences that matters most. Often the very differences that bring us together become annoyances after we are married. It is then that we begin our quest to change our spouse. However, authors Kiersey and Bates remind us, "There is no way to change our spouse into ourself. But the *attempt* to change the other is what does the damage. By chipping away on our spouse we say, 'You are not what I want. I want you other than you are.' Clearly what the spouse *is* is not appreciated, even though it is precisely what the spouse *is* that was the attraction in the first place." [7]

Some people are unwilling to live with differences. When they can't change their spouse, they give up on the marriage. Guilt and fear of divorce no longer serve as deterrents and they feel justified in looking out for themselves. Especially when they have given their spouse time to change and they don't see the desired results. Increasingly people are accepting the myth that they should expect perfect compatibility in their marriage. When it doesn't happen, they imagine that a "soul mate" is out there somewhere just waiting to be found. So why put up with something less than the best?

As happened with Pam and Mike, personality tests can exaggerate the importance of differences. Although these tests are intended to enlighten spouses about strengths and weaknesses, couples can misuse the information. In times of disagreement it is easy to drag out the findings from the tests. Armed with these conclusions, it is no longer just an opinion about our spouse; we have a test to prove it. How can we be comfortable with a person who is judgmental, insensitive, or any of the other negative words that describe their personality? Especially when the spouse refuses to accept what the tests say about them.

The Science of Personality

Perhaps the "science of personality" leads spouses to believe they can have a perfect marriage that is free of defects. In our success-driven society, science and the marketplace constantly promise a better life. Cures for diseases. Faster computers. And defect-free marriage. According to this logic, everything can be improved with enough effort and knowledge. So people who have grown accustomed to buying or working their way out of annoying infirmities assume that personality quirks can also be removed from their marriage. Or if that fails they can do better in another marriage.

Categorizing personality isn't just a recent thing. Hippocrates undertook such categorizing as early as 450 B.C. in ancient Greece! He thought people fit into one of four categories: melancholic, choleric, sanguine, or phlegmatic. Whatever you may think of those categories, there isn't much evidence that people paid attention to them then. They probably didn't even know about Hippocrates' ideas. After all, he couldn't explain them on radio or TV shows. Few people knew *what* type of personality they had.

Many other personality categories have been created in the twenty-five centuries since Hippocrates. They include the sixteen different personality types defined in the Myers-Briggs test. In this test, literally dozens of characteristics are clustered in categories that are very complicated and highly subjective. Does it help spouses to know that they are an INTJ or an ENTP? The Enneagram uses a numbering system to identify characteristics. But there, too, what does it mean to be identified by a number? And does this information provide practical help in marriage?

While tests can reveal some things about us that contain truth, the interpretations are often so general that they don't mean much. Some people fit into many of the categories, while some don't score high in any. Often the tests tell us some things that we already know about ourselves. According to Dr. Mary Pipher, perhaps the most damage is done to couples because ". . . .popular psychology encourages self-doubt, self-pity and self-absorption. It can give people labels rather than direction, and excuses rather than motivation."[8]

Furthermore, categorizing personality often draws our focus onto the negative qualities of our spouse. Even though the tests also reveal strengths, those are often overlooked. It is somewhat like the annual job performance review in which the supervisor points out the ten good things about the worker and the one area in which improvement is need-ed. Most workers obsess about the one negative and forget about the ten positives. As Dr. John Gottman suggests, "Measures of personality don't predict anything, but how people interact does."[9] We are, after all, much more complex beings than a number or a letter can adequately describe.

Mystery in Personality

When marriage is examined scientifically, it loses its mystery. Couples may know each other by their score on a personality test, but they may not know their score on the tests of daily living. While they may have learned some facts about *personality,* they may know very little about *character.* Pseudo-knowledge replaces genuine understanding. Besides, all of this self-inspection takes time and energy—precious resources that many people are lacking today. But some couples continue to "work" on their personality believing they will eventually "get it right."

So they read on and tune in. And attend one more retreat. They may even seek counseling. When all efforts to find marital perfection fail, some spouses give up, convinced that divorce is the only way to reclaim their dream. Many believe that a better match awaits them somewhere else. Some have already found another partner by the time they have declared the original marriage over. Pursuing the dream of perfection can continue on through several marriages. Eventually some people face the reality that the ideal partner doesn't exist. They even wish they had been more tolerant of the idiosyncrasies of the original spouse.

Sadly, many who over-analyze their marriage never live their marriage. The mystery of marriage is lost when they inspect the relationship too closely. These couples discard the comfort that comes from a continuing—if imperfect—relationship. They become obsessed with knowing the unknowable and changing the unchangeable. Marriage is as satisfying by what it is *not,* as well as by what it *is.* Thankfully, it is not constant ecstasy, but it is quiet security. It is not perfection; it is being loved in spite of imperfections. When couples learn to live within this reality, they experience the genuine pleasures of Monday Marriage. That is what intimacy is all about.

What Really Matters

When spouses aren't chasing after perfection, it frees them up to discover what they can really do to improve their marriage. Expecting too much is hurtful and so is giving back too little. If their problems come from work-related stress, for example, a job change may be necessary. If their troubles come from overfilled schedules, cutting back on activities may help. Some marriages will benefit simply by learning the art of compromise. Most couples could become more compatible simply by spending more time together. So instead of "working on the relationship," peace can come to their marriage when they spend quiet, unhurried moments with each other. Time together at the end of the day, a walk in the park, and an occasional week-end getaway can be amazingly curative!

To some extent marriage is a union of the improbable. A relationship of the unlikely. Examining it constantly under the microscope inevitably will find malignant cells. When couples accept their union as a sacred mystery rather than a laboratory experiment, the marriage will survive even with its defects. Indeed, marriage is an extension of God's love to us. God loves us even with our weaknesses and expects us to do the same for our spouse.

Differences bring vitality to a relationship, so rather than viewing those differences as our enemy, we need to embrace them as a friend. Indeed, we all need to make compromises—when possible—for the good of the relationship. Just as important, however, is that we show each other generous grace and forgiveness when change *can't* happen. The good news is that personality tends to modify over the years—sometimes by choice and sometimes through life experiences. Although couples on their fiftieth anniversary are somewhat like they were on their wedding day, they are also different in important ways. Much like the rugged granite cliffs on the Maine seashore, people are also changed by the tides.

When widows and widowers reflect on their years of marriage, they usually remember the small things in their relationship. The smell of coffee in the morning that their mate prepared, having someone to share a story with, the unique fragrance of a spouse. Sitting together in church. Taking the grandchildren camping. And a thousand more things. Rarely do they make reference to their letters on a personality test. When couples focus less on differences and more on what they have in common, they experience oneness.

There is no perfect personality and no perfect personality match. Searching for one takes couples on a futile journey that can only lead to disappointment. Rich, meaningful marriage comes from living within the reality of what is and what will continue to be. Monday Marriage is about acknowledging and negotiating differences. It is a celebration of the growth that comes from these differences. Monday Marriage is about a commitment to change the things that can be changed. It is also about accepting the differences that cannot be changed.

Many forces shape our personalities. Some are easy to define but most aren't. The human spirit is too complicated to fit neatly into categories. Monday spouses are content to live with the unknown and the imperfect. Their love for each other transcends the daily disappointments that come from human failure. Even though they will always see each other through an imperfect lens, couples draw comfort from knowing that—even with impaired vision—their marriage is a part of an eternal union with the Creator.

4

Being Realistic About Sex

TIM: I'm really confused. When we were dating she was all over me. She was the one taking the initiative most of the time. When we were first married, she seemed as excited as I was to have some variety in our sex life. I'd say we did pretty well until the first child came along. Then all of a sudden she changed. Sex was a bother and she seemed offended if I tried to put a little spark back into our marriage. I talked with our pastor and he suggested we go to a marriage retreat. The brochure he handed me used words like "ecstasy" and "sensuality" and promised to bring back the passion of the early years. Kim agreed to go but wasn't enthusiastic.

At the retreat we heard some famous speakers. Their wives told how they had lost sexual passion but got it back through hard work. The husbands learned to do nice, romantic things to make their wives feel appreciated. Things like candles, restaurants, and going away together overnight. They said it made their wives feel more cared-for. The wives even admitted they had to jump-start their passion even when they didn't feel like it. It made their husband easier to be around. And it worked for them. They seemed happy. It's really good to see people at their age excited about sex.

So we went home with a lot of hope. For a couple of weeks we had sex almost every night. It was like when we were first married. But then it went back to where it was before we went to the retreat. Worst of all it doesn't seem like Kim even cares. I sometimes wonder if Kim has a problem. All of my buddies say they have more sex than I do. Did Kim just put on a good front to get me to marry her?

KIM: I don't know what Tim's obsession with sex is all about. Yes, I know I had more interest when we were dating. But we're married now and we have a child. I'm up half of the night feeding our son and changing his diapers. Tim works long hours and seems preoccupied when he comes home. And then at ten o'clock he expects me to run upstairs to bed with him. I have to admit there are some times that I feel guilty for not going along with him.

After all, those women at the retreat did almost anything to please their husbands, and they seemed happy. Maybe there's something wrong with me. I saw a program the other day on TV about the low desire in many women. The doctor said sex could be much better if women just tried more. In fact, he said if we want to keep our husbands from having affairs we have to make it better. He used the same words that the speakers did at the retreat.

But I'm not sure I believe everything they say. In many ways it seems like a kind of game we play with each other. Sure, sex can be fun. Especially if there's a little romance in it. I do occasionally feel closer to Tim after sex. But I feel pressured to always make it into a huge event. Try new things, sexy nighties, different positions, daring locations. To "ooh" and "ah." Really, at times it seems like he expects me to put on a performance. And you know, by now most of the mystery is gone. I mean, Tim's a nice guy, and most of the time I even love him. But Tim's Tim. I know what he looks like with and without his clothes on. I know all of his habits. When he tries to woo me I know what's on his mind. In some ways it seems kind of silly.

The big thing is that we're both too busy to have sex, let alone the romance that I need. His long hours and my full-time career, getting our son to day care, and the committees we both chair at church leaves little time or energy for anything else. But when I think of it, maybe what kind of gets me mad about the whole thing is the big *should* that hangs over sex. I get it from everywhere. My friends, my doctor, and even my pastor. And I can't pick up a magazine in a waiting room without being told what I should be doing in this most personal part of my life. The message is clear. If we're to have a "good" marriage, Tim and I should have good—no, even great sex.

Sex Is Complicated

If sex is one of the basic instinctual drives that God gave us, like hunger and survival, then why do we have to work so hard at it? Shouldn't it just happen naturally and without anybody's help? After all, people don't have to be told how to get hungry or run from a burning building. So if it's such a powerful instinct, why do so many people say that sex is a problem in their marriage?

Advertisements to correct "erectile dysfunction" are everywhere. And why is Victoria's Secret important to so many people? What is Victoria whispering in our ears, anyway? It's puzzling that the most sexually liberated generation in history needs so much help with their sex life. But that doesn't seem to help couples like Tim and Kim. Couples have reliable birth control and all kinds of technical information about sex that their parents didn't have. The sexual freedom that exists now was expected to bring freedom from sexual "hang-ups." Conveniences like microwaves, computers, and hot tubs were supposed to give more time, energy for romance. So what has gone wrong?

The short answer is we expect too much *from* sex, and we give too little *to* marriage.

Expecting Too Much

It is hard to be realistic about sex when we live in an environment that hypes everything—especially sex. The Olympics and the Superbowl are made into colossal events even though we are often disappointed with the outcomes. Blockbuster movies are promoted shamelessly. Advertisements make products irresistible. Everything in American life is based on making things bigger, better, and more exciting. Americans are frequently reminded that they are the world's remaining Superpower.

So can exaggerated expectations for sex be far behind? As psychiatrist John Jacobs notes: "We are inundated with images of endless sexual activity in ways that were never feasible or imaginable even in the recent past. . . . We long to experience the same excitement for ourselves, and when we don't, we're easily disappointed."[10] These images of sexual activity greet us at the check out counter of our local grocery store, invade most TV programs, and are even hyped in some Christian literature. Against that background, it is no surprise that many of us are easily disappointed with our sex lives. Jacobs believes that sex has become one more commodity in an economy that is influenced by a "media circus."

The Hippie Movement of the late 1960s helped create this sexual revolution. The "new morality" removed boundaries that had been in place for generations. Sexual pleasure became a right and focused on personal gratification. Sex became a mainstream topic of discussion and was no longer something to whisper about. Sexual freedom became a public fact of life. Nudity soon became widely accepted, from Broadway musicals to *Playboy* magazine.

This change about the way sex was viewed affected the marital bedroom dramatically.

At about the same time, science entered the scene. Gynecologist Dr. William Masters and psychologist Virginia Johnson became household names as a result of their laboratory studies of human sexuality. They charted orgasms and collected sexual fluids. They put names to the various dysfunctions and created therapies aimed at correcting them. Because these technical discoveries were shared widely through the media, many couples began to expect much more from their sex life. They learned how to make their bodies work better and in turn felt entitled to sexual fulfillment. The marital bedroom became an extension of the Masters and Johnson laboratory.

This emphasis on sex has made some spouses focus excessively on technique and performance. Some are painfully self-conscious about their ability as lovers. Spouses increasingly wonder how good they are in bed. Compatibility and mutual pleasure—every time—has become the gold standard for couples. This new information raised unrealistic expectations and has made sex into an act of physiology more than a natural expression of love.

In the midst of this revolution, the divorce rate began to climb. Alarmed pastors, counselors, and well-intentioned "experts" became convinced that good and frequent sex would be the main prevention and remedy for marital problems. They talked about building an "affair-proof marriage." Good sex was thought to be a part of keeping marriage strong. Some leaders suggested that it would be the "super glue" that holds marriage together. But sex as remedy has never worked when the problems outside the bedroom aren't solved. No amount of hype—or promises to prevent divorce—can change that fact. It is much more helpful to present realistic information to couples about their sex life, and to help them to correct what is really wrong in the first place.

Giving Too Little

At the same time couples expect too much from sex, they get themselves in trouble by giving too little attention to their relationship. Many couples have problems simply because they choose the wrong priorities. They make choices that deprive the marriage of its time and energy, taking the focus away from where it should be. These problems will never be fixed simply by convincing couples to have more and better sex. If marriages are to survive, the following ideas will be important:

Don't allow our jobs to control our marriage. For many of us, there simply isn't enough time or energy left over from our jobs to fulfill the needs of marriage, including sex. Any quick-fix answers won't come until we deal more effectively with what work can do to marriage. This means preserving time at home for the relationship. It is important to plan for the occasional work-free, distraction-free evening.

Put boundaries around high-risk friendships. It is essential to place boundaries around male/female relationships that occur outside the marriage. The greatest threat now comes from workplace friendships. More than 65 percent of affairs are between fellow workers. They may start innocently through sharing personal information, water cooler conversations, office related parties, and other ways. At work—and all other places where we have frequent contacts with other people—spouses need to be aware of the risks to their marriage and keep clear limits in place. When friendships outside marriage become more important than the relationship with the spouse, the marriage is placed at risk.

Commit to preserving free time with the spouse. Cut back on free-time activities. Marriage suffers from being too busy. Many couples lament that they don't have enough time for each other sexually or otherwise. Taking a critical look at the family calendar may produce some surprising answers. Frenzied spouses make poor lovers.

Maintain realistic lifestyle priorities. Houses are becoming larger and more expensive to maintain. Depending on elaborate vacations to resolve sexual problems often leads to disappointment. The impulse to purchase more gadgets and paraphernalia becomes a burden. These and other excesses are present at all income levels and take the focus away from the marriage. We do better at marriage when we keep things simple. An appropriate lifestyle makes space for intimate marriage.

Monday Marriage, Sex and Intimacy

We hope you have given up unrealistic ideas about sex and that you are working on new priorities for your marriage. When we make major changes in our expectations and in our choices we are in for a big surprise: intimacy! Until now we have deliberately been talking about sex because that is what most people focus on first. Indeed, sex is something most of us want. But intimacy is what we all need. Unfortunately, too much sex in marriage is only *sex*. That is why many people like Tim and Kim fight about it. And why some people escape into pornography or into affairs. What they really are searching for is intimacy, not just better sex. When people are intimate, the sexual part usually works just fine.

Dr. Willard Krabill says, "True intimacy means being with another person in a way that is closer than the contact of two bodies (that, incidentally, is no big accomplishment).

It is the interaction of those persons in a relationship of knowing and trusting that is closer than just the physical." He goes on to say, "To develop true intimacy takes lots of *time*. It is a process, a dynamic, growing experience. There is no instant, easy way to experience true intimacy, despite what the soap operas, movies, and songs may tell us."[11]

In Monday Marriage intimacy is never an isolated event that takes place in a bedroom. Intimacy happens in the context of carrying out normal adult responsibilities. Sometimes alone, more often together. Raking leaves, cooking a meal. Reading bedtime stories for the children, taking them to the zoo, or helping them catch their first fish. Intimacy happens when both spouses comfort an ailing parent, or help neighbors who have financial troubles. Intimacy is much more about an attitude of *giving* than it is about *getting*. When spouses show this kind of agape love, it ignites within them the deepest feeling of intimate love for each other.

Spouses who are at peace with themselves and with each other are more creative in their lovemaking. Their sensuality will be expressed in the ways they touch, talk, and are present with each other. Intimate partners take down their guard and create a spirit of total acceptance. Nothing is more intimate than giving each other undivided attention, undistracted passion, and unconditional love. Indeed Monday Marriage partners can engage in passionate sex. God put the excitatory neurotransmitters in the brain for a reason. Maybe for many reasons. But exciting sex can only happen when first there is exciting intimacy.

But *you* need to fill in the blanks on how that is expressed in your life. In this chapter we are deliberately avoiding a cookbook formulation for sex in your marriage. There are too many of those ideas floating around already in books and other places. Many trivialize intimacy by laying out a plan for touching each other's bodies or by giving lessons in human anatomy. That may sell books or captivate an audience. But these presentations make spouses into body mechanics or performers on a sexual stage. Worst of all, they miss the real point of intimacy. Intimacy isn't about the body. It is about the soul.

Your ways of being intimate belong to you. Intimacy isn't invented by some author or speaker at a seminar. When you remove unrealistic fantasies from your expectations, you will discover the deep, satisfying passions that come from being in the arms of your life long spouse! You will experience intimacy when you see in the eyes of your spouse the understanding that can only come from years of shared joy and pain. We invite you to discover loving intimacy within the realities of Monday Marriage. Relish the quiet moments together when little is said and nothing is touched but your soul. The soul, in the end, is the most intimate organ!

5

Communicating Imperfectly

KAREN: To be honest, I left my husband for another man because he just didn't know how to communicate. When my husband and I were together on a trip he could go hours without saying anything. At mealtime I always had to keep up the conversation. Sure, he talked about his work but that was so boring. And he never seemed interested in what I was feeling. Then, BAM, I met this great guy at work and found out what good communication was. The first night we were together we talked nonstop until three in the morning. And we're still going strong. I know if we get married, communication will be the most important thing in our life.

KARL: I know I failed Karen by not talking enough. But words don't come as easy for me as they do for her. When we were dating, Karen said she was so much in love that it didn't matter. And I did talk more back then but she often interrupted and took over the conversation, so I backed off. We talked about our dreams, having kids, building a house, and having friends over. You know, I still have the love letters we sent to each other and some of the cards we gave for birthdays, anniversaries, and on Valentine's day. If we weren't communicating perfectly, we must have been doing something right. Now that she's in an affair I think her memories are twisted.

Communicating Is Hard

It is hard to communicate well. Words often fail us in one way or another. We use the wrong words, talk too much, or not enough. We are too superficial or too philo- sophical, too romantic or too stoic. Even the Bible recog- nizes that words can be misused when it identifies the tongue as "a double-edged sword." In Karl's situation he apparently didn't use enough words or the right words to please Karen. But maybe her pattern of interrupting him or acting bored by his stories was discouraging to him. Most of all, she probably expected too much from him, especial- ly now that she compares him to her lover. Communication during affairs is intense, but can be misleading. People in affairs often mistake passion for good communication.

It is easy to understand why so many people are unhappy with their communication. Just watch the popu- lar TV talk shows for a few minutes or pick up your favorite magazine. The message is loud and clear—poor communication seems to be a national epidemic! This mes- sage suggests that virtually everyone needs a communica- tion coach to have a successful marriage. To find answers to this problem, scientists like Dr. John Gottman study the subject in laboratories. Among other things, he charts the heart and breathing rates to understand the physical con- nection for couples who are in conflict. He calls this the "CAT scan of a living relationship."

Because of this focus, some couples have become more concerned with their *methods* than with their *message*. Their heart rate more than their heartaches. With marital communications under the microscope—and with expec- tations so high—it isn't surprising that people like Karen have trouble connecting with their spouse. This intense public focus has given some people the idea that they are entitled to high-quality communication in marriage, much like they might feel entitled to receive Medicare when they turn sixty-five, or to be given a refund on a defective product. In that sense many spouses demand good communication from each other. When that expectation isn't met, some seek it from someone else.

Let's look at some ways that spouses can become more realistic about communication:

Use fewer words. Some spouses believe that if they use lots of words they are communicating well. Whether talking about mundane or serious matters they ramble on. They especially ratchet up the words during conflict, thinking it will help resolve the problem. But it usually makes it worse. After a certain point fatigue takes over and the conflict becomes hurtful. In a society that floods us daily with megabytes of information we assume that quantity means quality. That is, the more we talk the better we are communicating. In reality, when the brain is swamped with information, *none* of it is useful.

We need to practice good verbal stewardship by developing an economy of words. That is, to not be so quick to use words. And to separate the important from the unimportant. It is necessary to learn the skill of silence. To take delight in enjoying the presence of each other, maybe while we are watching a sunset or taking a walk together. The preacher in the book of Ecclesiastes reminds us that there is "a time to keep silence, and a time to speak" (3:7). We would all do well to know when—and when *not*—to speak. It is often when we aren't speaking that we usually are thinking. It is then that we become the most clearheaded. Mark Twain would go even further. "There are times," he said, "when I like to sit and think. And there are other times that I like to just sit." Many marriages would do well to follow his advice.

Place less emphasis on using the right words. Some couples have become so cautious about the way they speak that much of the spontaneity is taken from their communication. They have gotten the message that choosing their words carefully is very important. So they walk on tiptoes around each other for fear of saying things the wrong way. They are coached to use "I messages" to convey personal feelings ("I feel upset when dinner isn't ready") and to avoid using "you messages," ("you make me feel upset when you never have dinner ready when I come home").

They get bogged down in artificial communication. It is tedious and time consuming. Some, like Karl, withdraw because they don't want to make a mistake. He is somewhat intimidated because Karen appears to be a more skillful communicator. This kind of imbalance is hard on marriage and can drive wedges between spouses. It is unfortunate that the obsession with correctness has made some people afraid to talk with each other. Choosing words carefully may be necessary for diplomacy between countries or in a legal document. But the health of marriage should not depend on the exactness of our words.

Certainly, none of us should intentionally hurt a spouse with words. Most of us can be much more affirming. Indeed words are important in marriage. They are needed to convey information, feelings, and dreams. Words can be enlightening, humorous, and entertaining. They should be rich in spontaneity and wonderfully unselfconscious. Our words should free us, not bind us. Mistakes and blunders in communication can even enrich relationships.

"Enrichment" happened to Marlene and me one time

when we were canoeing with our teen-age daughters on the Au Sable River in Michigan. I was giving Marlene some uninvited advice on her rowing. She was annoyed but tolerant. When we needed to take the canoe out of the river to get around a dam, we communicated—but not well enough! To my surprise she got out of the front of the canoe before I was ready. The canoe tipped over and I ended up in the river. When I came to the surface I found Marlene and our daughters enjoying "dry humor" from their comfortable perch on the bank of the river. Needless to say we both found better ways to communicate the rest of the way!

Place less emphasis on "deep communication." Some spouses believe that marital communication is only valid if it is heavily laced with words from the great writers, philosophers, scientists, or politicians. They may even expect discussions about their faith that are deeply theological and ponderous. Some want the communication to be richly romantic or to reach the depths of the psyche in search of *the inner child*. To them the normal marital chatter about daily events seems like useless noise.

Karen—and other people like her—mistakenly believe that marital communication should always be deeply personal. Most of us have our moments with our spouse when communication is intimate and energizing. We treasure those moments deeply. These times are an investment in the relationship that pays long-term dividends. Marlene and I often find these moments when we are on long trips in the car. The phone isn't there to interfere. The doorbell doesn't ring. We're not fixing anything or anybody. We cry, we laugh, and we dream. Most of all we allow epiphany— that unexpected discovery of something we never thought of before—to happen.

But it's a mistake to expect that to happen all of the

time. Not even daily! Indeed, Monday Marriage is maintained by the ordinary conversations we have about day-to-day events. That is where we really live. That is what we need to talk about. When we expect—even demand—that the daily discussions be filled with emotion, passion, and intensity, we will be disappointed. It can't happen routinely in Monday Marriage. And it doesn't need to. Daily conversation is the verbal cement that keeps spouses in touch with reality—and with each other.

Do not expect both spouses to have the same communication style. In reality, few spouses communicate the same way. Talkative people tend to marry quiet people. Emotional people tend to marry reserved people. The way we communicate is a direct extension of our personality and maybe even our gender. It is amazing that with so much emphasis on respecting diversity in our culture, we still expect everyone to communicate in the same way. School children are coached to speak uniformly through speech classes and other performance-driven tasks. And premarital couples are often taught communication "skills," as if there is one preferred way to communicate.

Needless to say, we are different in so many ways, including the ways we speak—or don't speak. Yes, we can all do better. We all get lazy and careless and a little prodding can help. But no cookie-cutter remedies to make us all talk the same will work. God makes us different for a reason. If we believe the myths about perfect communication we set ourselves up for failure and disappointment.

Expecting less from "listening skills." Indeed, it is important for spouses to listen carefully to each other. Perhaps nothing is more disappointing than speaking to someone who is obviously tuning us out. You can see it in their eyes and can tell it by their words. Jesus was the ultimate listener. He waited patiently and responded appropriately. Compassionate attention is one of the best gifts we can give each other. It feels good to be heard!

But there are realities that we all have to live with as speakers and listeners. We have many distractions, some of them unavoidable. And many times when we try to listen we are genuinely fatigued. In addition, listeners don't always have the same interest in the subject that the speaker has. To expect listeners to be completely attentive all the time isn't realistic.

Even though in the counseling setting, couples may learn to repeat back what the spouse has just said as a way to improve listening skills, it is hard to do in marriage. It takes time, is cumbersome, and makes the marriage clinical. Certainly couples need to ask each other clarifying questions and use words that confirm what the other has just said. But techniques that are used in a counselor's office may be difficult to use at home. Besides, what we *see* during a conversation is often more important than what we *hear*. Perhaps the most important listening skill of all is touch. Nothing can be more clarifying than a gentle embrace or a hand that is tightly held.

Monday Communication

If you're expecting perfect communication with your spouse, come down out of the clouds. Put aside the book that is raising your expectations too high. Turn off the TV or radio. Cancel your reservation at the retreat center. Welcome to Monday. It's not such a bad place to be. It's where you live most of the time. Maybe your conversation is often about the daily routine and may seem meaningless. However, if you are realistic and treasure the many wonderful ways you communicate with your spouse—imperfect as that may be—you'll do just fine.

Remember that we communicate in many ways. Some of those ways are with words, but most are not. Often our actions and our priorities communicate more powerfully than any words can. Choosing to remain sexually faithful says a great deal. Treating each other with respect is often done without words. Touch, when done in love and without strings attached, has tremendous power to communicate. A simple smile or acknowledgment goes a long way. All of these types of communication require no particular skill. Nobody should have to attend a seminar to find out how to do them. Monday people communicate well without thinking. These ways to communicate are central to what we believe and who we are.

The best communicators are those who are totally present with each other in body, soul, and spirit. They give undivided attention to each other with their eyes, ears, and mind. They are not multi-tasking. They are not rushing the moment. Their TV and computer are turned off and their newspaper waits to be read at another time. Undivided attention is the gold standard for marital communication.

Most of the time marital conversation will be about the routine, mundane details of life. Sometimes it will be about things that are urgent. The most meaningful communication can happen when nothing is said at all! In the end, communication is much more about *attitude* than it is about *method*. Humility and compassion will yield more benefit to the marriage than the superficial skills presently offered to couples.

Monday people communicate with their feet firmly planted in the realities of daily life. They have come to peace with their own limitations and those of their spouse. They take special comfort from knowing that they share a special bond that began with words but has now gone beyond words.

Part Two

Giving More

6

Honoring the Marriage Covenant

Fred is a man on the move, a successful middle-aged businessman with lots of admirers. He is repeatedly elected president of his service club, serves on fundraisers in the community, and is a deacon in his church. He lives in a nice house in a good neighborhood. Every aspect of his life is going according to plan. Everything, that is, but his marriage. For years he has felt rejected by Millie. She refuses to go along with him to public events. He has had to make excuses for her absences. When she is with him in public she is short-off with people and clearly is a smudge on his image.

At home things are even worse. She is critical of him, refuses affection, and often stays away from him when he is around. For years, Fred has remembered his mother's warnings that he and Millie weren't a good match, in part because she thought Millie's own family wasn't stable. When Millie stopped going to church with Fred, he began to wonder if he would be better off divorced. He was worried what that might mean to their two teens, but on the other hand he believed the marriage wasn't a good model for them.

Eventually, Fred consulted a lawyer and was about ready to move out when he felt a gnawing feeling in his stomach. Memories from their courtship flooded in. They had fun together, talked about everything in depth and even were affectionate. Yes, they were different, but Fred didn't believe this would matter in the long run. He dismissed his mother's warnings; she had always been critical of his previous girlfriends. He felt God had brought he and Millie together, and he wanted to lift her out of an unhappy life.

Memories of their wedding kept flooding in: Millie, so attractive in her gown; people coming from near and far to celebrate with them. And the vows. How could he forget the vows? They worked hard to write and memorize them. "Millie, even though we come from different backgrounds, I know that through Christ we can become one." "Fred, I love you because of your strength and I trust you to keep your promises." And more. With tears in their eyes the minister acknowledged their vows and warned that no one should cause the marriage to be broken. They had made a covenant "before God and these witnesses" to be together "until death do us part."

Did he really mean what he said then? He was only twenty-five, and Millie has since become impossible to live with. He talked with friends and most told him to leave because the love was gone and Millie wasn't even trying. If divorce was wrong it was certainly forgivable. So move on, Fred. You've got half of your life ahead of you yet.

But Fred could not set aside his vows. They were more than just a promise. More than just a legal contract. He had made a *decision* to love Millie forever. The covenant he made with her was also with God and with the people who were at the wedding. So he tore up the papers the lawyer had prepared and instead made an appointment with a Christian counselor. He was persuaded to take a hard look in the mirror and not to focus so much on how Millie had failed him. It was then that he discovered that *he* had abandoned Millie. His pursuit of his own interests took him away from her. Fred remembered his sacred commitment and changed his priorities to not let anyone or anything come between them. With these changes, Millie responded warmly to her new husband. Joy and intimacy returned. The covenant was the anchor that kept them together.

Taking Commitment Too Lightly

For many people, it seems commitment to marriage doesn't mean much anymore. Many give up too quickly. On the other hand, some have no choice because their spouse abandons them. Others leave for their own protection. For many, however, the idea of honoring a commitment is a concept that is outdated, perhaps a hang-up from an overly religious past.

In the present culture, couples are given many "acceptable" reasons for breaking up. "We're incompatible." "He doesn't meet my needs." "I'm in love with someone else." "She's an addictive spender." "He's a tightwad." "She's a compulsive talker." "He's a couch potato." Or the more psychologically sophisticated, "My marriage was too confining. It kept me from reaching my potential." So when some couples are unhappy in their marriage they give up, citing "irreconcilable differences."

In some ways marriage has become an extension of dating. That is, couples stay together only until they have a falling-out, get tired of each other, or until somebody better comes along. Could this indicate that the maturity level of couples has gone down? That is ironic when the average age for marrying has *gone up*! Studies show that some people have become more self-centered. When it comes to making personal sacrifices they aren't willing to compromise. Author Pamela Paul notes that twenty percent of all marriages today end within the first five years. The idea of being committed to a covenant doesn't seem to matter much to these people.

The Role of the Church in Supporting Covenant

Covenant is a sacred promise. The church has a unique role in giving meaning to covenant. It has often done well in helping divorced people by providing them with support groups and pastoral counseling. On the other hand, the church shouldn't abandon its role as an advocate for covenant and permanence in marriage. It can be the light on a hill that advocates permanence in marriage through preaching and teaching, modeling, and moral persuasion. Don S. Browning and others, in their study of marriage in the Christian church, found that covenant is a powerful symbol that "evokes commitment."

The Israelites posted the Ten Commandments on their doors, on their foreheads, and their wrists as reminders of their relationship with God. In a similar way, many of us wear wedding bands as a reminder of our marriage. Perhaps we should also display our marriage license and a copy of our vows prominently in our homes. Some churches have an annual ceremony for couples to renew their vows. Whatever those powerful symbols may be, we need to search for new models that support maintaining marital permanence.

Influences from Society

We are all influenced by the world we live in, where nothing is forever and rapid change is the only certainty. Computers become obsolete in a year or two. The hardware store we shopped at most of our life closes when the box stores come to town. And the church where we were baptized is barely able to survive because most members have moved on to the megachurch down the road. Change, it seems, is inevitable. Could it be that permanence in marriage is no longer important?

Pamela Paul has concluded from her research that ". . . satisfaction with married life decreases significantly after the first five years; in our accelerated society, it follows that this bliss period will shorten. We may have neither the patience nor the willpower to wait it out. We who are so accustomed to and enamored with speed may not understand that marriage is a series of developments, a never-ending process that is meant to last—GASP—longer than college or our last job. We could be coveting something we're simply not equipped to sustain."[12]

Giving to Marriage

If we're really serious about saving marriage we need to discover what we can do *for* our marriage, not what we can get *from* it. That means honoring our covenant by changing both our attitudes and our actions. For most people maintaining the commitment to our spouse is a choice that can be shown in several important ways:

Choose a lifestyle that supports maturity. Popular culture is built around what appeals to the lowest common denominator. TV "reality shows" exploit the participants and the audience by their sexuality and vulgarity. Pop music with regressive lyrics invites listeners to prolong adolescence. Many couples escape into fantasy and denial believing they don't really have to settle down. Maybe never! Increasingly, couples are making lifestyle choices that are similar to those of adolescence. Mothers try to dress and act like their daughters. Fathers hang out with their buddies like their sons do with their friends.

If we are serious about our covenant we will develop a

lifestyle that supports maturity. We will slow down our pace, reduce the volume of the noise around us and focus on things that really matter, especially the well-being of our marriage. And not just for the short run, but for a lifetime. We will choose to be strengthened by mature models in our church and our community. Mature couples will be enlightened and entertained in ways that have lasting value. "Growing up" means accepting responsibility, including commitment to marriage.

Seek spiritual depth. Fred recommitted himself to Millie. His relationship with God and the influences of his church were the foundation upon which his marriage was built. When we take our faith seriously, all decisions we make in our life reflect our spiritual commitment. We don't just abandon a spouse and children because we want to. Not even because others say we should. We uphold our covenant because it is a sacred promise to God. Spiritual depth means that we seek to grow in our understanding of—and relationship with—God just like we do with our spouse. We pray with an attitude of openness in ways that strengthen marriage.

Eugene Peterson finds meaning in his life through the call to worship. "Every call to worship," he says, "is a call into the Real World. You'd think by this time in my life I wouldn't need to be called anymore, but I do. I encounter such constant and widespread lying about reality each day, and meet such skilled and systematic distortion of the truth that I'm always in danger of losing my grip on reality. The reality, of course, is that God is sovereign and Christ is Savior. The reality is that prayer is my mother tongue and the Eucharist my basic food. The reality is that baptism, not Myers-Briggs, defines who I am."[13]

Marriage requires humility and acts of service. Selfishness and arrogance are common reasons marriages come apart. Before Fred looked in the mirror he was headed for failure. He was driven by competitiveness, external success, and self-indulgence. Author Paul Pearsall refers to this combination as "toxic success." Not only is it damaging our health, he says, but it's also destroying our marriages. On the other hand, Pearsall adds, "Sweet success is first and foremost the experience of loss of self and freedom from constraints of time and self protection and enhancement."[14] Some of the motivational seminars Fred attended emphasized achieving *personal* goals. Humility, loss of self, and service weren't on the list.

Author and preacher Wellington Boone has a wonderful answer to this problem. He begins every day with the goal of out-serving his wife. When he wakes up, he resolves to win a contest to do more for her than she can do for him. He is aware of the power that being a male brings him. He tries to be "like Christ" in the attitudes he displays in his marriage. "We are happier, more peaceful people," he says, "when we are more concerned with what we give up than with what we get."[15]

Covenant is needed because we are imperfect people. We wouldn't need to promise anything if we were perfect. In Fred's case he came into marriage expecting imperfection in Millie. His mother had duly warned him. His main mistake was not coming face to face with *his own* imperfection until the marriage was in trouble. Indeed, Fred, Millie—or any of us—could theoretically find a *better* match with someone else. We might spend the rest of our lives looking, and even then the better match wouldn't guarantee a better marriage. But that's not the point. The real issue is that none of us can find a *perfect* match.

Because of our *imperfection,* we need the boundaries provided by our covenant.

In a free society, where couples—totally on their own—choose a mate, the "best" matches won't always occur. It is interesting to note that our family doctor grew up in Bangladesh, where marriages are arranged by parents. Even though she used to see this as an archaic system, she now wonders whether parents are indeed better matchmakers than impulsive, hormone-driven couples!

Philip Yancey adds that in societies where marriages are arranged, "After your parent's decision, you accept that you will live for many years with someone you now barely know. The overriding question changes from 'Whom should I marry?' to 'Given this partner, what kind of marriage can we construct together?'"[16]

Celebrating Differences

Monday Marriage accepts—indeed, even celebrates—differences. God made us all different, so it becomes a matter of accepting the differences. Fred honored his covenant by changing his priorities and humbling himself. The differences between he and Millie no longer mattered. Because he changed, Millie's negativity began to change. Monday spouses don't care so much about these differences, but care a great deal about their commitments. It is in the security of covenant that they find comfort, acceptance, and joy. It is the only way to experience true intimacy. Covenant is much more than a legalistic ball and chain around the ankles of spouses. It is the key that opens the lock and gives them true freedom.

Perhaps the greatest strain on the covenant comes when a spouse has a significant mental illness or an addiction. These conditions can place a heavy burden on spouses. But many of these situations can be modified with counseling and/or medication. It is when people refuse to seek help that they place their marriage at risk. When couples work together to deal with these challenges, many are able to maintain a rich, meaningful life together.

Covenant serves as our anchor in marriage because it keeps us connected to God and each other. Covenant helps us avoid impulsive, selfish choices. In a spirit of humility and service we submit to God, our faith community, and ultimately to each other. We seek maturity to strengthen our covenant. In Monday Marriage we work at understanding our differences and are strengthened by them. Most of all we enjoy marriage as a sacred bond that can only take place within the covenant relationship.

7

Keeping Work in Its Place

Perhaps nothing else has more influence on marriage than the work we do. It demands a major portion of our time, energy, and allegiance. It often gives us an identity that carries over into marriage. While work can be very fulfilling it can also cause great stress and frustration. The warning, "Caution: Work can be hazardous to marriage" should be posted on the door of every workplace. On the other hand, when we lose our jobs—or retire—some people also adjust poorly. Some get depressed, even to the point that they become abusive to their spouse or children. Work has a powerful influence on us.

Most of us *have* to work to provide income. And many of us *choose* to work because it is a creative way to express our gifts. Some people work because it gives them a sense of power, prestige, and privilege. Whatever the case— noble or otherwise—work affects marriage. Sometimes for the better. Sometimes for the worse. Let's look at some of the ways work can influence us.

Work makes us physically and emotionally tired. Often when we return home from work, we are physically and emotionally spent and have little energy left over. If the workday was filled with stress, hurtful emotions are often carried into the home. Work stress can damage our marriage. Tired and frustrated workers tend to be irritable,

73

argumentative, or detached when they arrive at home. Work-related stress and fatigue is often overlooked because, to a degree, it is inevitable. But when it affects our health and our marriage significantly, we need to calculate the true costs of what it is doing to us.

> Hal has a high-pressure job as a computer analyst/programmer. He solves problems for a far-flung corporate computer network. Many people depend on his ability to fix glitches that prevent them from getting accurate data quickly. And most of the day his attention is spent staring at a monitor in an isolated work cell. In some ways that fits his personality because he has never been a chatty, social person.
>
> So when Hal gets home in the evening his "tank" is empty. He is tired, frustrated, and emotionally distant. The problem is that Meg needs him. All of him. When she tries to share her daily woes and triumphs, he sighs and evades her eyes. He still has million dollar problems on his mind and finds it difficult to get interested in their child's potty training troubles. Meg gets the message that she doesn't matter. As the weeks and months go by, Meg ends up discouraged and feeling hopeless. Hal has trouble raising the energy level for her.

Work can take a great deal of time. Most spouses work outside the home. The two-income family has become common. Many spouses are required to work overtime, some work different shifts, and increasingly spouses bring work home with them. Recent studies show that couples work, on average, a combined ninety hours per week. Many people now commute longer distances to their work. Increasingly the global economy is requiring sacrifices from workers. Television ads show them on the beach—supposedly on vacation—while working on their laptops or communicating by cell phone with the home office. Work is increasingly squeezing marriage into the margin. Clearly, couples today have less time for each other as a result.

Parkinson's Law says, "Work expands to fill the time available." Kaufman's Law says, "Marriage suffers as the time available for it contracts," as the following case shows:

> Cindy is a nurse in a busy emergency room at the local hospital. She is dedicated to her patients and consistently gets good evaluations from her supervisor. She likes her work, although she is well aware that she frequently comes home exhausted. Because of the nursing shortage, she frequently stays late or covers evening and weekend shifts. Being a loyal worker, she serves on some hospital committees. When other nurses want to change their days off, Cindy is often willing to accommodate, even if she had already made plans with her husband. Because she has no children, Cindy believes she has no excuses for not putting in extra time. Consequently she averages more than fifty hours per week.
>
> Mike enjoys the big paychecks Cindy brings home because the money has enabled them to buy a nice house and take special vacations. But he is starting to feel restless. He is tired of "hanging out" with his single friends and is beginning to feel distant from Cindy. When he complains, she says they spend "quality time" when they are together. But Mike isn't convinced that the "quality" is enough to make up for the lack of "quantity."

Work can test faithfulness to our spouse. Men and women now often work alongside each other. Virtually every kind of job can be filled by either gender. While that can enrich the workplace and open up opportunities for women, it can pose a threat to marriage by leading to inappropriate friendships. Many of these friendships become affairs.

Sociologists have long known that propinquity—that is, being physically near to someone—tends to foster friendship. The risk becomes greater when workers travel together to conventions or on other work-related trips. Even company banquets or parties create risks when spouses aren't invited to attend. Attractions can develop because workers often look and act their best in the workplace. At home we tend to "dress down and act up"! Our spouses see us for who we really are.

Workplace friendships don't have to be romantic to be a threat to marriage. When workers frequently spend time together over lunch, after work, or on weekends—in some cases sharing vacations—the relationship with the spouse can be weakened. This shifts the primary focus away from the spouse and often leads to sharing personal and intimate information outside the marriage, as this case demonstrates:

> George was in his late fifties and an executive in a medium-sized company when he became restless. While he was able to avoid some of the common signs of getting older, his wife, Sarah, wasn't. He jogged, lifted weights, and kept his body in good shape. He enjoyed the attention he got from younger women. It was partly his position in the company that conveyed power, but it was also the way he looked. At least that is what he thought.
>
> Menopause, too many snacks, and too little exercise left Sarah looking somewhat matronly. George continually pleaded with her to lose weight. Sarah reminded him that he married her "for better or for worse." Besides, wasn't all that romantic stuff over by now? George failed to recognize that his long hours at the office and on the road left Sarah feeling lonely and neglected. And affected her motivation.
>
> Their problems were made greater when George became attracted to a young, divorced administrative

assistant. Because of their roles in the business, George and his assistant had a great deal of contact, some of it in his office with the door closed to discuss confidential business details. They took trips together to conventions. And soon, they began staying late to finish "desk work." What started out as a very effective working relationship gradually changed into a personal one. It soon became a full-blown affair that threatened his marriage.

Work gives us an identity that can conflict with our role as a spouse. Work often requires us to play a role that is very different from the role we play at home. We tend to define ourselves by what we do at work and carry that identity home. Thus we are truckers, sales reps, teachers, or businesspersons more than we are husbands, wives, fathers, or mothers. Our work roles not only tell people what we do, but more importantly define who we are. Most of all they influence the way we act in marriage. Our work personalities tend to become our marital personalities. Therefore if you are a CEO of your company, you could tend to be a CEO at home.

But imagine yourself as, say, a trial lawyer yet not arguing a case with your spouse over which car to buy, or how to discipline the children. Or if you are a schoolteacher, imagine not using your "teacher voice" with your spouse. We've heard it said that some counselors have been known to be psychoanalytic with their mate! Amazing how much our job influences us when we get home. These work roles are so deeply ingrained in us that we have to *intentionally* set them aside at the front door.

> Tom is a young police officer and his wife, Tina, is a social worker. When they return home after work it is hard for them to change roles. Tom speaks in his clipped, terse voice as if still on duty. His demeanor usually conveys an expectation for conflict. It is as if he

expects an assailant to jump up from behind the sofa. Planning for their weekend trip to the mountain sounds more like a military maneuver than a romantic getaway.

Meanwhile Tina is tentative, asks lots of "why" questions, and wonders how Tom feels about nearly everything. He wants to move ahead on things promptly and without much discussion. Tina is more comfortable processing their decisions and discussing their relationship. He is more concerned with the destination and she with the journey. But when Tom remembers he has taken his uniform off, and when Tina no longer talks to him as she would with a client, they are able to become husband and wife once again. Those are the only roles that work in marriage.

Giving Back to Marriage

Work is one of the main reasons we give too little back to marriage. It can rob us of our best time and energy. It can bring intruders into our relationship in the form of excessively close friendships, affairs, or misplaced loyalties. Work gives us an identity that is often harmful at home. Among other things, work can make us selfish, materialistic, and ego-driven. For some spouses work can give a handy excuse for escaping from marriage.

Up against these powerful forces, what's a good Monday person to do? Certainly not stop working. We need to pay the bills. And we work to perform the many tasks that are needed in the world around us. Perhaps most importantly we work to express our God-given creative gifts.

Monday people set boundaries around work that protect marriage. For them, work is an extension of their marriage, not something that controls the marriage. Perhaps most importantly, they limit the duration of—or even avoid altogether—jobs that are known to be hard on marriage, especially those that:

- Require extensive travel without time-off compensation.
- Consistently require large amounts of overtime.
- Are overly stressful for the worker's physical and marital health.
- Have few boundaries for interpersonal friendships.
- Imprint an identity on the worker that conflicts with marriage.

It is impossible to avoid all risks that come from our jobs, but we can do better. Because jobs are necessary to support our lifestyle, few people question the demands of the workplace. So bit by bit, we make concessions and the marriage suffers as a result.

Monday spouses are alert to what work is doing to their marriage and take the necessary steps to protect it. Those steps include deciding if a two-income marriage is wise during the early stages of child-rearing, whether to make business trips with workers of the opposite sex, what part alcohol will play in work-related activities, and resisting the excessive demands of the employer. Perhaps, most of all, spouses will resist attitudes of power and self-centeredness that can come from their role at work.

Monday spouses are good workers. They choose their work carefully and they manage it conscientiously. At the end of the day they return to each other knowing that they have done something worthwhile. They are thankful for the privilege of doing good work. Out of that richness they are better persons and their marriage is energized by what they have done. At the same time, the security of their marriage is protected by the ways they have placed boundaries around their work. Above all else, Monday spouses are committed to the sanctity of their marriage and the integrity of their faith.

8

Taking Control of Free Time

Jack and Chris had begun to argue a lot. Even over little things. It took them by surprise because they thought they had a good marriage. Many of their friends looked up to them as an ideal couple. They were active in the church where they were youth advisors. Jack coached his son's little league team. Chris served on the board of a center for single mothers.

When middle age left her out of shape, Chris enrolled in a ballet class. She took her daughter along with her to feel less guilty for being away from the family. It worked. She felt rejuvenated. In addition, her instructor encouraged the daughter to continue with ballet because she showed "outstanding potential." She was winning contests and receiving the loudest applause at recitals. The instructor recommended that she come to the studio three nights per week. So Chris used this opportunity to work out at the same time.

Much to her surprise Jack began to grumble about the added time at the studio—not to mention the expense. Things around the house were being neglected. Dishes were left in the sink, frozen pizza was becoming a staple, and the family meal had become a distant memory. There was little energy left for the relationship. When Chris announced that their daughter had been invited to a month-long ballet class in New York—and that she would go with her—Jack became angry. He and the marriage had been stretched too far.

How We Are Busy

There is evidence everywhere that we are too busy. While none of us should sit around idly, we are talking here about being *too* busy. Just follow a "soccer mom" who picks up her child after practice and has to hit all of the traffic lights just right to arrive at her son's little league game on time. She then hurries home to make dinner.

Watch her husband, who spent a few hours at work early on Saturday morning before playing in a golf fundraiser and then rushed off to take the daughter to music lessons. After dinner Jack spent the evening preparing a speech that he was to give to the Rotary club. If these stories sound familiar it is because they are common to many of us. There's a consensus that we're too busy. Most people believe, however, that there is nothing they can do about it. So our marriages have become casualties of schedules that are out of control.

Sometimes we blame it on the children's activities, but adults find plenty of ways to be busy all on their own. Whether it is golf, bowling, tennis, or many other forms of recreation, we find ways to overspend our free time. While exercise and recreation are important, they need to have some boundaries around them.

There are many other ways to be too busy. As committed members of our church, we teach Sunday school, serve on committees, and reach out to families in need. In our communities, we help with the chicken barbecue to raise money for the volunteer fire department, or assist with service club projects. We help our aging parents, mow our disabled neighbor's yard, and work on a Habitat for Humanity crew, and the list goes on and on. All of these activities are worthwhile but can push the marriage into the margins.

Some people use up their free time being entertained by TV, attending sporting events, plays and concerts, or by going to movies. Surprisingly, some studies show that shopping is what makes us the most busy! Studies show we spend an average of six hours per week shopping.

The newest competitor for our time is the computer. People increasingly devote time each day traveling the "information highway," playing interactive games, and corresponding by e-mail. Some individuals get hooked on computer pornography. Somewhere we also have to find time to pay our bills, make meals, do the laundry, clean our cars, and to mow the lawn. And because we have much more "stuff," it takes longer to maintain our homes. Again the marriage takes a back seat.

Having Too Many Choices

We are too busy, in part, because we live in a society that offers too many choices. In his book *The Paradox of Choice*, Dr. Barry Schwartz notes that we are asked to choose from 275 different kinds of cereal, 175 types of tea, dozens of forms of entertainment, telephone options that confuse us, and on and on! All of this takes precious time to figure out. Still, we insist on having as many choices as possible, even though these choices make us busier than ever.

Making choices has become a major drain on our time and our energy. Yet the more options we have, the less happy we've become. Dr. Schwartz discovered that people with too many choices report "a significant *decrease* in well-being."[17] This smorgasbord of choices burdens us in many ways, as this story illustrates.

A friend tells us about the time his daughter had just returned to the United States after spending several years teaching in China. Beyond the usual readjustments to North American culture, one in particular stood out. One day, when he and his daughter were grocery shopping, she went looking for bottled water while he picked up some other items.

After what he thought should have been an adequate amount of time, he went back to the bottled water isle and found her in tears. Somewhat shocked, he asked her about her sadness. She explained that there were simply too many choices and she was overwhelmed. After living in a country where choices were far fewer and less complicated, she just couldn't decide.

Children and Busyness

Our children's activities help to make us too busy. Apparently we allow that to happen because "everyone else" is doing it. It seems to be contagious. We don't want to be the only parents on the block to keep kids out of year-round soccer, even if it means missing family meals, church on Sunday, or postponing vacations. The same thing happens with baseball, basketball, and other competitive activities. Peer pressure on children and parents can be very powerful. It is hard for parents to think objectively about their priorities.

We involve our children in these activities for many reasons. Some people do it believing it will prevent delinquency, drug and alcohol use, and will help build character. Others hope their children will acquire enough skill to compete in the Olympics or professional sports. At the very least, parents hope their child will be good enough to get a full athletic scholarship to a university. Most parents don't set goals that high, but may have a personal investment in their child becoming a "winner" in their hometown. However, devoting so much time to such goals rarely pays off. The number of children who "make it to the top" is very small, and even hometown celebrity tends to fade quickly. Parents need to be more realistic about what their children will gain—and what they will lose—from competitive activity.

Many parents want their children active to keep them from being bored. Our culture suggests that every moment of a child's life should be filled, and that somehow idleness is harmful to character building. But as columnist Anna Quindlen points out, it is when our children are doing "nothing" that they "do their best thinking, and when creativity comes to call." "Downtime" she says, "is where we become ourselves, looking into the middle distance, kicking at the curb, lying on the grass or sitting on the stoop and staring at the tedious blue of the summer sky."[18]

Adult Busyness

Some of us choose busyness for ourselves because it makes us feel important. Did you ever notice the tone of voice in people who say how "crazy" their schedule is? They attempt to feign regret but more often reveal that busyness makes them feel significant. "Oh, I'm sorry we can't go out to dinner with you. It looks like the schedule for the next two months is just jammed!" Or, "I just can't take on one more assignment because my wife says the kids will forget who I am!"

Many of us have mixed feelings about our busyness. On the one hand, we know we should be home more. On the other hand, busyness can be addictive. Some people actually get a little burst of adrenaline when they run from here to there, or from one meeting to the next. They tend to walk faster through the foyer at church or find satisfaction from being the last person to leave a meeting. They get a lift from seeing their picture in the paper following an important meeting. Others feel validated if the phone "rings off the hook" or upon returning from vacation find the e-mail box filled with messages.

We probably are too busy because we are afraid of "nothingness." Influenced by a society that rejects an unscheduled moment, we run from it like it is an enemy. While we were on vacation Marlene noticed a mother at the swimming pool who—during a thunder break—promptly offered three options to her children for what they could do during the mandatory thirty-minute time-out. It was as if the children couldn't figure it out for themselves and that unscheduled free time would be harmful to them. In our culture, we associate busyness with goodness, maybe even godliness. A lack of busyness with laziness, mediocrity, and boredom.

How Being Too Busy Affects Marriage

Busyness—even busyness that comes from doing "good things"—can weaken marriage because it takes time, energy, and focus away from the relationship. Marital intimacy can never be rushed or pushed into the margins of marriage. But when intimacy seems lacking, spouses complain and blame each other for the failure. Many look for quick fixes through sexual enhancement pills, artificial stimulation, or high-voltage weekend escapes.

Few pause long enough to discover the real cause—busyness! What we say we want often fails to match what we are willing to do to get it. At the same time we are frustrated with our lack of intimacy, we trudge off to another bowling league, antique show, and football game with the old gang, or whatever. Few of us don't see the connection between our lack of intimacy and our busyness. So we have our "love affairs" with that old car we are restoring;

we run to one more basket party; or we waste one more Sunday watching football. And go on complaining!

Excessive busyness usually affects us both physically and emotionally. Fatigue causes the release of stress hormones that are harmful and depletes health-producing brain chemicals needed for wellness. Some of the most hurtful conflicts between Marlene and I happen when we are too busy. I get grumpy and Marlene grumps back. We say things we later regret. Usually we do poor problem-solving at these times. Almost without exception, couples who have frequent conflict are swamped with stress hormones. Busyness can literally be toxic to marriage.

Busyness and Monday Marriage

Many of us complain about being too busy. But we believe there is little we can do about it, so we allow others to decide how we spend our free time. In a society where busyness is epidemic, few people give much thought its effect on marriage. But busyness is a *choice*. If our free time is really free, that means it belongs to us and we need to decide how to spend it. Monday Marriage people protect their marriages from the damaging effects of busyness. We will control the schedule because we know nobody will do it for us.

We take control by scheduling time for the marriage each week. Five hours, ten hours, something. We schedule everything else that is important to us, including our jobs, curch services, and appointments with the doctor. Doesn't marriage deserve as much? Many people resist scheduling time for their relationship because it seems artificial and removes spontaneity and surprise. What would the neighbors think if they see us sitting on the porch? What will the coach say if "our time together" interferes with bringing our children to practice? Besides, what will we *do* during the time together? Won't we get bored? If time together isn't scheduled, the odds are that nothing will happen. Scheduling creates an expectation that something good will happen.

We protect against busyness by selecting our activities carefully. Many activities don't deserve our time. They have marginal value to our children or to us. Typically they take more *from* us than they return *to* us. You might say their cost-benefit ratio doesn't favor marriage. It is important to question activities like year-round soccer for our children, ballet lessons three nights per week, playing on two softball teams, working out at the gym every night, and lots of other things that control our lives. We need to be especially critical of "noble" activities like the committees we serve on at church or in the community. How many meetings have you come home from wishing you hadn't attended? If you have, it's time to think of resigning from the committee or to suggest more structure for the meeting.

We accept help to solve our busyness problem. We may need accountability partners. That can be another couple who shares our commitment to marriage, a counselor, or a friend. If we are in a small group at church, we should ask the members to review our busyness regularly. Some people might need busyness-addiction recovery groups!

Busyness addicts might need what people in the recovery movement call "interventions" in which family and friends around the addict to confront them with their addiction. Pastors should conduct an annual busyness audit with members to help them be more aware of its impact on their lives. Busyness can destroy people and marriages. If the church is *really* concerned about marriage it needs to lead the way in advocating Sabbath from busyness.

It is in our time of Sabbath that we reconnect with our spouse. We rediscover the person with whom we fell in love, the person with whom we intended to do so many good things. It is only when we reject the merchants of busyness that we are able to reclaim the intimate bond we have neglected. So we walk together, sit on park benches, throw stones into sparkling streams, gain perspective from the mountaintops, or relax on the patio. We pray, cry, laugh, grumble, imagine, and dream. We enjoy apple fritters together. Nothing fancy or exotic. Just the humble expressions of Monday Marriage. It is through experiencing Sabbath that we discover "nothing" is really "something." We can never make those discoveries when we are too busy.

Epilogue:
Monday Morning

A Homily

It's eight o'clock Monday morning. Do you know where your marriage is? The school bus is waiting at the front of the house. One of you has already left to run the Marketplace Marathon. The other is lacing up running shoes. And the marriage is headed for another week of rain delays and postponements. The World Series and the Superbowl of your marriage will surely be played. Sometime. Just not now. That will have to wait.

But not to worry. As graduates of the school of popular psychology you know about Perfect Marriage, Terrific Marriage, and Ecstasy Marriage. You even know how to build an Affair-proof Marriage. You may not feel a surge of enthusiasm about your marriage today, but you take enough continuing-education courses to keep the dream alive.

You are running the race, but you haven't finished the course. Maybe tomorrow. Maybe when the busses no longer come. Maybe when the mortgage is paid off and you can take jobs that aren't so demanding. The hot tub and the whirlpool will still be there waiting. You comfort yourself, convinced you will use them. Sometime. You've heard that if you are going to have your dream marriage, you simply have to want it enough and work hard enough to get it. You convince yourself that you will, too. After soccer is over. When you get off the committee.

Isn't it true that people who put in enough effort always win the big prize? You've heard from the big guys that Monday Marriage is mediocre. That it is for losers. Winners have Winning Marriage. So let's get to work. We'll accomplish personality compatibility at week's end by taking an assertiveness class to improve our self-esteem. By the end of next week, it's Winning Sex when we awaken those old excitatory neurotransmitters that have been sleeping. Indeed, we'll have Winning Communication before the month is over by using more "I messages" and "reflective listening."

We're convinced Winning Marriage is there waiting for us. All we have to "just do it." Now where did we put those Nike shoes? Must have misplaced them again. Maybe we'll have to wait until next month to get the winning streak started. This *is* the busy time of the year. And then there's Christmas. Maybe we should wait until next year. Yes, next year. We can be winners anytime we want to.

Welcome to Monday morning. And to the comfort that comes from living within reality. Despite our disappointments, we are enriched by the unfailing trust and permanent commitment of Monday Marriage. Acceptance of imperfection validates it. It is driven much more by *we* than by *me*. Monday morning is the true measure of marriage. It is when we step across the threshold of maturity. Who of us, after all, can live in the perpetual weekend? Or be an all-the-time winner? We surprise ourselves by discovering that Monday Marriage is real. It is sustainable. It is renewable.

It is on Monday morning that we experience the true meaning of intimacy. Monday is about being at peace with ourselves, our spouse, and our Creator. Nothing fancy, glitzy, staged, scripted, or starry-eyed. Monday never puts us in categorical boxes or hands out workbooks that end up gathering dust. It is intimacy lived in all of its undramatic richness.

Monday morning is survivable because it flows seamlessly from the rest of our life. It isn't the start of a five-day parenthesis in the marriage. Monday people are also Friday people. And Sunday people. Monday Marriages aren't segmented by time, place, or identity. Monday spouses aren't one person on one day and another person the next day. They aren't overcome by desires to remodel each other into something more to their liking. They have long ago given up looking for the "perfect match."

Monday people gain a lot from doing nothing. Or what looks like nothing. They are enriched by looking off into the middle distance. They treasure apple fritters and whistling *before and after* their spouse is gone. They desire to occupy the same space physically, emotionally, and spiritually. They make a choice to be aware of each other. They are tuned in to what they can see, hear, touch, taste and smell in their relationship. These senses inform their soul about an outer adult that they can really know. Not an inner child that they can't.

Monday people dignify each other by keeping the promises in their sacred covenant. "Setting aside all others"—including work, ambition, and activities—they "cling to each other and become one flesh." Most of all Monday people are content with what they *do* have, and long ago gave up pursuing what they *don't* have. Monday people are content in whatever state they find themselves.

It's Monday morning, and you know where you marriage is. It's been inside you all along. It has never left. And you've never left to pursue impossible dreams, or to be obsessed with winning. Distractions from work have never taken Monday Marriage from you. Play has never come between you. You have not been abandoned for the mirage of somebody better.

In your faithfulness to God, you have been faithful to your covenant. In your submission to each other you have conquered your separateness. Imperfect as you may be, you are blessed by the intimacy that only comes from truthfulness and unconditional love. Laughter and tears are your great reward. Your memories are a sacred scrapbook. Your future is filled with hope. You have the joy, intimacy, and security of Monday Marriage.

Notes

1. Miller, *Eyes at the Window*, 252-53.
2. Gundy, *Scattering Point*, 31.
3. Schwartz, *Scientific American* (April 2004): 74.
4. Shulman, *Psychology Today* (March-April 2004): 34.
5. Jacobs, *All You Need is Love*, xii.
6. Covington, *Salvation on Sand Mountain*, 204.
7. Kiersey and Bates, *Please Understand Me*, 68.
8. Pipher, *The Shelter of Each Other*, 112.
9. Gottman, *Psychology Today* (April 2004), 53.
10. Jacobs, *All You Need is Love*, 205.
11. Krabill, *Sexuality, God's Gift,* 56.
12. Paul, *The Starter Marriage*, xvii.
13. Peterson, *The Wisdom of Each Other*, 110.
14. Pearsall, *Toxic Success*, 275.
15. Boone, *Your Wife is Not Your Momma*, 2.
16. Yancey, *Reaching for the Invisible God*, 271.
17. Schwartz, *The Paradox of Choice*, 108-09.
18. Quindlen, *Newsweek* (May 13, 2002), 76.

Bibliography

Boone, Wellington. *Your Wife is Not Your Momma: How You Can Have Heaven in Your Home.* New York: Doubleday, 1999.

Browning, Don S. *From Culture Wars to Common Ground: Religion and the American Family Debate.* Louisville, Ky.: Westminster John Knox Press, 2000.

Covington, Dennis. *Salvation on Sand Mountain: Snake Handling and Redemption in Southern Appalachia.* New York: Penguin, 1995.

Glass, Shirley P. *Not "Just Friends": Protect Your Relationship from Infidelity and Heal the Trauma of Betrayal.* New York: Free Press, 2003.

Gottman, John. "The Truth About Compatibility," *Psychology Today* (April 2004).

Gundy, Jeff. *Scattering Point: The World in a Mennonite Eye.* Albany, N.Y.: State University of New York Press, 2003.

Jacobs, John W. *All You Need is Love and Other Lies About Marriage.* New York: HarperCollins, 2004.

Kaufman, Gerald W., L. Marlene Kaufman, Anne Kaufman Weaver, Nina Kaufman Harnish. *Freedom Fences: How to Set Limits That Free You to Enjoy Your Marriage and Family.* Scottdale, Pa.: Herald Press, 1999.

Kelley, Linda. *Two Incomes and Still Broke? It's Not How Much You Make, but How Much You Keep.* New York: Random House, 1996.

Kiersey, David, and Marilyn Bates. *Please Understand Me: Character and Temperament Types*. Del Mar, Calif.: Prometheus Nemesis Book Co., 1984.

Krabill, Willard S., "The Gift and Intimacy" in *Sexuality, God's Gift*, edited by Anne Krabill Hershberger. Scottdale, Pa.: Herald Press, 1999.

Kraybill, Donald. *The Upside-Down Kingdom*. Scottdale, Pa.: Herald Press, 1978.

Marano, Hara Estroff. "The Truth About Compatibility" in *Psychology Today* (October 2004).

McQuilkin, Robertson. *A Promise Kept*. Wheaton, Ill.: Tyndale, 1998.

Miller, Evie Yoder. *Eyes at the Window: A Novel*. Intercourse, Pa.: Good Books, 2003.

Paul, Pamela. *The Starter Marriage and the Future of Matrimony*. New York: Villard Books, 2002.

Pearsall, Paul. *Toxic Success: How to Stop Striving and Start Thriving*. Makawao, Hawaii: Inner Ocean Publishing, 2002.

Peterson, Eugene H. *The Wisdom of Each Other: A Conversation Between Spiritual Friends*. Grand Rapids: Zondervan, 1998.

Pipher, Mary. *The Shelter of Each Other: Rebuilding Our Families*. New York: G. P. Putnam's Sons, 1996.

Quindlen, Anna. "Doing Nothing Is Something," *Newsweek* (May 13, 2002).

Schwartz, Barry. *The Paradox of Choice: Why More is Less*. New York: HarperCollins, 2004.

———. "The Tyranny of Choice," *Scientific American* (April 2004).

Shulman, Polly. "Great Expectations," *Psychology Today* (March-April 2004).

Swenson, Richard A. *Margin: How to Create the Emotional, Physical, Financial and Time Reserves You Need.* Colorado Springs, Colo.: Nav Press, 1992.

Thomas, Gary. *Sacred Marriage: What if God Designed Marriage to Make Us Holy More Than to Make Us Happy?* Grand Rapids: Zondervan, 2000.

Yancey, Philip. *Reaching for the Invisible God: What Can We Expect to Find?* Grand Rapids: Zondervan, 2000.

About the Authors

Gerald W. Kaufman, LCSW, BCD, holds a bachelor's degree from Goshen (Ind.) College and a master's degree in social work from Indiana University. He has been in private practice since 1974 and has worked as Chief Social Worker at Philhaven Hospital, and in the Department of Psychiatry at Penn State School of Medicine. He was born in Johnstown, Pennsylvania, and has lived and worked in Akron, Pa., since 1980.

L. Marlene Kaufman, LCSW, BCD, holds a bachelor's degree from Goshen College and a master's degree in social work from Temple University in Philadelphia. She was born in Dewey, Illinois. In 1980, Marlene and Gerald founded Kaufman Counseling Service. Their practice serves individuals, couples, and families. They are members of Akron Mennonite Church.

Gerald and Marlene have enjoyed nearly forty-five years of ordinary marriage and have helped many couples over the past two decades as professional marriage counselors. They have led many workshops about marriage and family life issues and are the authors, along with their daughters, of *Freedom Fences: How to Set Limits That Free You to Enjoy Your Marriage and Family* (Herald Press, 1999).